7/30/90

DO NOT REMOVE
CARDS FROM POCKET

TOGETHER

Till
Death
Us Do
Part

JOHN M. BRAATEN

Twenty-One
Wedding
Meditations

C.S.S. Publishing Co., Inc.
Lima, Ohio

TOGETHER . . . TILL DEATH US DO PART

Copyright © 1987 by
The C.S.S. Publishing Company, Inc.
Lima, Ohio

SECOND PRINTING 1989

Library of Congress Cataloging-in-Publication Data

Braaten, John M., 1938-
    Together — till death do us part.

    1. Marriage — Religious aspects — Christianity — Meditations. I. Title.
BV4278.B73   1987   242'.64   86-28336
ISBN 0-89536-852-8

7811 / ISBN 0-89536-852-8   PRINTED IN U.S.A.

Dedicated to my beloved wife, Julie, who
has made our marriage beautiful and thus has
made my preaching about it so much, much easier.

Table of Contents

Foreword

Writing a foreword is like introducing a friend. Therefore one must have made friends with the book before consenting to write. These are some of the reasons why I have made friends with this book of wedding meditations.

It is a needed book. In a time when the glaring lights of cynicism and sentimentalism threaten to blind our eyes whenever the subject of marriage is mentioned, we need a clear, steady light from God's Word if we are to experience Christian fulfillment and maturing joy in our marriage relationships.

It is a celebrative book. It is exuberant and festive in spirit even as it shows a mellow realism in relation to the responsibilities and stern tests of marriage.

It is an honest book. It bears witness in human terms to the author's personal experience of joy in the marriage relationship and the rewards which come with the passing year of devotion to one another.

These meditations help us to hear the voice of the Christian community, as it gathers around the marrying persons to undergird and support the commitments which they make. They express the embrace of the family of faith and the warm affection of the pastor and congregation.

It must be noted, too, that a saving sense of humor with reference to big and little crises is everywhere evident in these lines. And the writing is singularly free from repetitiousness, even though all of the meditations deal with the same general subject.

Read, not only to celebrate one event in living, but to be nourished in your Christian life as a whole.

— Gerhard Frost

Introduction

Writing meditations is challenging when you officiate at fifteen to twenty weddings a year and the entire community shows up for every one, including one person who takes notes! The pastor must be constantly on the alert for new ideas. While funeral sermons abound, special occasion sermons are everywhere, stewardship sermons are plentiful, and pericope homilies are a dime a dozen (although they cost much more), usable wedding material is difficult to locate.

There are reasons for this, to be sure. First, wedding meditations are, in my opinion, the most difficult sermons to create. Therefore, once a pastor has accumulated a *stable* of effective messages, he is reluctant to share them.

A second reason for the dearth of published marriage meditations is suggested by the comment of a man who came up to me following a wedding. He said, "I want to shake your hand. This is the fourth wedding I've been to this month and you're the first pastor that had anything worthwhile to say."

It is difficult for a pastor to find enough time to adequately prepare for these momentous family events. But they are times of *kairos* and we should not mouth *sweet nothings* into the ears of those assembled. We must translate the beauty of the Gospel into the vernacular. That is our vocation.

Thus I have set myself to the task of providing a resource for pastors and other interested parties. The sermons herein have all been preached to my patient people. Some of the meditations are very personal. In "The Crisis of Marriage," the bride and groom were approaching the altar for the second time; both had lost their first spouses to cancer. Other themes have been suggested by the bride and groom. For instance, "Together . . . Till Death Us Do Part," followed a request for a *real sermon* at the wedding. Still other messages are seasonal; "The Joy of New Beginnings" was preached at a wedding on New Year's Day. But behind *every* work is the proclamation that marriage is designed to be lifelong. In nearly every case the meditations are tied into Holy Scripture, for that which we tender to newlyweds (and their guests) is not to be merely good advice — it is to be *Good News.*

This manuscript owes its existence to many persons: To Dr. Gerhard Frost, my mentor and friend, who gave me confidence that

I could write some "worthwhile stuff," and whose prodding motivated me to get started. To members of my family, who loved me even when I stayed late at the office, working. To Pastor Scott Tunseth, who served as consultant and, along with Chaplain Art Johnson, provided enough *strokes* to keep me going. To Myrna Lyng, whose proficient proofreading and editorial suggestions were greatly appreciated. To my text study comrades, who encouraged me by hinting they might even buy my material if it were published. And to countless unremembered persons, whose writings ignited my imagination and inspired me when my own creative flame was flickering.

I pray that this book may in some small way serve others, as a nudge in the direction of proclaiming the glory and goodness of God, who designed that wonderful and most intimate of all relationships — marriage.

J. M. B.

Prologue

Author's Note: Every once in a while an occasion presents itself which gives rise to something unique. The wedding of a professional artist to a professional musician was such a time. Although this meditation has no scriptural text, it is biblical and serves as an exposition of my *theology* of marriage.

Metaphores of Marriage

"Into the bonds of Holy Matrimony come this man and woman now to be united . . ."

And on . . . and on . . . the parson drones, as though not quite aware of those two worlds embodied — standing now before him.

The adult-children, oh so innocent of what love costs — and of the greater price required if love is lost.

For, latent in the history of each, lie all the possibilities for human drama: of tragedy or comedy — of terrible grief or joy.

Look deep within their eyes, O man of God; what see you there? Of hopes — of fears — what festering wounds, what fantasies?

Drink deeply of the Holy Spirit's power and pray; for what occurs before you on this day is not a simple ceremony — child's play.

In this momentous moment, dies are cast and lines are drawn. Eternity breaks into life.

For these two persons, having touched each others souls, can nevermore return to innocence.

From this time onward, till eternity, this union bears the marks of its creation.

From this time onward, all their words and deeds become ingredients within the crucible of their united life, and from this cauldron ever streams life's sweet aroma . . . or the stench of death.

From this time onward — in wedded bliss or rueful separation — their persons never can be severed from this day — this act.

For God has said, "From this time onward, these two shall become one."

II

The scene now shifts, and what we speak of here is not, "What if . . ." or "Let's pretend."

The personalities enfused and inextricably entwined today are not the lives of persons make-believe.

Today the Lord God says, you, __(name)__ and __(name)__, shall become one.

And thus before you lies the future and the choice, of struggling against this unity, or celebrating love within its mystery.

But what does marriage really mean?

And how is beauty born within this bond?

Our God has said that you are one, and yet he also says that you are singular, unique.

Can this one solitary act, one set of vows, miraculously change all you have been?

To search this meaning, let us say you two are melodies with different beats, in different keys.

Now each of you, until this time, has used your days composing your life's theme to make it lovely and complete.

God calls you not to change your monody, to rearrange all that you are into one shared and single tune.

But rather set your minds on harmony, that through your giving in and giving up — in compromise — create a polyphonic rhapsody of beauty rare.

And all the overtones developed thus will radiantly surround both you and those you love with happiness and warmth.

But as you know, life's not that simple, quite. Its myriad motifs, merged with the selfish surety of will, produce jarring tones and discordance, and in their wake, the rhythms clash and harmony dissolves.

So in that hour recall our Lord, who on a Cross sang out the agonizing aria of grace.

His love — so undeserved — he offered, offers freely to us all.

And if, in imitation of his love, you dare forgive, then through forgiveness Christ can modulate all strident strains, until they blend once more in music strong, mellifluous, and sweet.

And then play on — point, counterpoint, descant — it matters not.

The Holy Spirit will transpose your feeblest lays into a mighty hymn of praise to God.

III

So very soon you two will venture forth into the dawning of a brand new life.

Like artists each, you stand, palette in hand, with brushes poised to paint.

But now you do not work in solitude, or create portraitures in just your style.

Your task — from this time on — will be the lifelong mural of your future shared.

Begin by knowing all the colors that you hold; for every hope and expectation, every dream is represented by a pigment and a hue.

And only as you know each other's spectrum as your own can you proceed unerring to your goal.

Then study carefully the style of your mate, for every bride and groom begin as dilettantes.

And even a full lifetime spent cannot reveal all of the wondrous modes and details of your beings.

But if you seek contented happiness once you are wed, then listen closely, for there's no greater truth.

Take time, consider, ponder well the final panel of the picture that you share.

For though the fresco of your life will be created day by day, existence has momentum toward eternity.

And knowing that you share a common faith allows you freedom; then you'll trust each other as to composition, balance, shades, and tints.

Or let us put it in another way: Our Savior, Jesus Christ once said, "Seek first God's kingdom, make your peace with him; then all you really need will come to you as well."

If faith can lead you two to say, "Amen!" then go and joyfully put on your artist's smocks.

Sketch in your fondest dreams . . . your hopes . . . and confidently paint with strokes both strong and bold.

But sometimes throw away your plans and fling your colors at the sky, and with abandoned glee, make all the universe a gaudy, opalescent sea!

For God is great, and through his Son, our Lord and Savior Jesus Christ, he'll add his touch of grace — transforming all you've done — and daily make your marriage blest . . . a masterwork of love!

Marital Horticulture

(Name) and _(name)_ we have gathered together this afternoon just for you. We have come, at your invitation, to hear you express your love for each other and to witness the making of your sacred vows. We are thrilled for you on this beautiful day as you step into the future as husband and wife.

We are mindful that fantasy is usually involved in thinking about a wedding. However, marriage is not a whimsical experience. So I ask you, and forgive me if it sounds brutal, "So what?" So what if your wedding today is a beautiful affair if, in a year or in ten years, your marriage withers and dies? So what if you are today caught up in ecstasy, if at some future day you find yourself regretting this very hour? The questions may seem unkind, but they are realistic. Almost one out of every two marriages ends in divorce. As one cynic put it, "If marriages are made in heaven, God's doing a pretty lousy job these days."

Of course you and I know that marriages aren't made in heaven. They're made on earth by young and sinful human beings. And unless the persons who make up a relationship are willing to sacrifice, to work *for* each other, and to forgive one another, their marriage will certainly fail. Romance cannot hold a marriage together. Only unselfish love can do that.

Let me illustrate by means of a homely parable. A couple goes out to plant a seed: a seed which, they hope, will grow into a beautiful and healthy plant. The seed is lovingly cared for as it is sown. It is watered and watched over anxiously. Then one day the seed germinates. It breaks the ground, thrusting its leaves upward. What a day of celebration! The flower is growing. Then, seeing that the plant is established, the couple leaves it to itself and no longer attends its needs. Soon weeds close in, garden pests attack, and diseases infect it. Because the plant lacks sufficient water and nutrients, it slowly but surely shrivels and dies.

You have probably guessed by now that the parable is really the story of a love relationship. When two people become serious about each other, the seed of love is planted. During courtship they foster that love. They feel anxiety over their relationship and strive to make it grow by pleasing the other. Then comes the wedding day. The seedling of their love breaks the ground and their love becomes public in a wedding ceremony. But the *plant* of their marriage must be cared for if it is to survive. Unless the weeds of selfishness, pride, and mistrust are rooted out, the marriage will have to struggle to grow. Unless the diseases of pettiness and stubbornness are arrested, the marriage will never become as beautiful as God designed it to be. Unless the marriage is exposed to the sunlight of love and affection, it will become stunted and weak. Unless it is generously nourished with words of forgiveness and encouragement, it will surely die.

You see, _____ and _____, the seedling of your love has just broken the surface on this day. Today is not the culmination of your romance; it is but the beginning. All you have done, all you have meant to each other; has been preparation. The growth of your marriage, and its blossoming into beauty, will depend upon what you do from this day forward.

As your family and friends, we have great hopes and dreams for your marriage, just as you do. But we know that wedded bliss doesn't just happen. You will have to work hard in the garden of your marriage if it is to grow and flourish. That is why I suggest you take the psalmist's words to heart: "Blessed are those who fear the Lord, who walk in his ways! You shall eat the fruit of the labor of your hands; you shall be happy, and it shall be well with you." Psalm 128:1-2

These words are not intended as crop insurance as much as they are words of gardening advice from an agricultural expert. He knows what he's talking about. He advises you to stay close to God. For God's presence in a marriage is like water to a plant. He comes to shower receptive hearts with unique and rich blessings. In experiencing his forgiveness and love we are motivated to be forgiving and loving toward one another. We know that plants grow best in warm weather. Only God can add the warmth that will make the *plant* of your marriage grow lush and beautiful, its fragrance embellishing the lives of all who are touched by it.

Make no mistake. The cultivation of your marriage is still up to you. Even if marriages were made in heaven, they would still need to be lived out on earth. In marriage, God gives you the responsibility for the care and keeping of the other. You are to love, forgive, share, and communicate his great love. In a sense, God's love takes on human form through your relationship as husband and wife. It is an awesome responsibility, but it can be a great joy, and it can make of your marriage a flower of wondrous beauty, one which is able to decorate the world for the glory of God.

So we urge you never to forget your responsibilities toward each other on behalf of your Creator and Redeemer. And I commend these words to you as you leave this place to begin work in the garden of your marriage: you will be blessed, _____ and _____, if you live respectfully before the Lord and walk in his ways. You will eat the fruit of the labor of your hands. You will be happy, and it will be well with you.

To that end, God bless you today and forever. Amen

Marriage as Gift-giving

   (Name) and   (name) , as you stand here in the front of the church, it may feel like you're *onstage,* and indeed you are. All eyes are upon you, and all hearts are beating with yours in the excitement of this much-anticipated event. But in truth, we are all on stage. We are participants in the Service of Worship you have created to honor our Lord, as he comes to bless your new life together.

   You designed this worship experience to praise God for all he has done for us through our Lord Jesus Christ. It is your response to the good news that God gave his only Son as a free gift to redeem us. It is in this spirit of gift-giving that we listen to Paul's words from Romans: "I appeal to you therefore, by the mercies of God, to present yourselves as a living sacrifice, holy and acceptable to God, which is your spiritual worship." Romans 12:1

   Paul says we are to dedicate our lives, offering them as gifts to God. In other words, we are to commit our lives to God for a holy purpose. It is only natural that this commitment spills over into our lives and into our marriages. So giving ourselves sacrificially to God includes submitting ourselves to each other on our wedding day. We are to be *gift* to each other and we must learn to receive each other as *gift.*

   A gift is a surprise package, infinitely less than we expected, and infinitely more than we ever dared to dream. To receive another as gift, we must first make room in our heart and life for that gift. To make room for the gift is to clean house, ridding ourselves of assumptions, needs, and demands. It is to say to our beloved, "I have room for you as you are, as you want to become — not as I think you should be. Come, you will experience space and safety with me. I will receive and cherish you, just as I wish to be received and cherished."

To receive each other as gift means to daily honor the freedom, and not the ownership, of the gift. A gift is always freely given, always something received that we have not earned. It can never be paid for. You are gift to each other: a gift to be valued, not evaluated; to be cared for, not controlled; to be protected, not possessed; to be discovered, not exploited.

You know, when something is purchased it is new only once. Soon it wears out and needs to be replaced. The gift of self, however, has the potential to be renewed daily, with brand new facets and neat surprises. Sound too good to be true?

I recall attending a sixty-fifth wedding anniversary in my first parish. Trying to be humorous, I said to the *groom,* "It must get pretty old living with the same person for over sixty-five years."

His eyes blazed, "Listen, if I don't discover something new about my wife every so often, I know I've been thinking about myself too much."

Wow! But you see, the sacrificial giving of one's self brings the wonder of unexpected depths. Over the years, this gift grows richer, and more precious in experience. Ultimately it becomes irreplaceable and priceless: it becomes love incarnate. And then the two become so intertwined that the gift and the receiver are, in fact, one!

Finally, not only do we give ourselves freely, but we receive each other freely. It is like grace which loves for the sake of loving and asks nothing in return. So, in receiving the gift we are to open our hearts and our hands, to allow our fences to come down, and to include another in our dreams and journeys. To become a gift-receiver means to think not only of one's self, but always to include the other: to create communion, to know community, to be a family, to experience home. To receive another as gift enables a marriage to unfold so one must use such *inadequate* words as affection, trust, tenderness, forgiveness, faith, one flesh, to describe that relationship.

_____ and _____, as you give yourselves as gift to

each other, and freely receive each other as gift, you will find yourselves revealed, known, appreciated, understood, and rejoiced in!

So it is the prayer of those who love and care for you, who hope you will enjoy the greatest of marriages, that you will be gift and gift-receiver to each other, thus duplicating, in a mysterious and marvelous way, the gift which God gave us in his Son, Jesus. In so doing, you will serve our Lord through each other to the glory of God. Amen

One from Two

(Name) and _(name)_, on this your wedding day, grace to you and peace from God our Father and from the Lord Jesus Christ. Amen

If I read Scripture correctly, today you two will become one. For our Lord said: "Have you not read that he who made them from the beginning made them male and female, and said, 'For this reason a man shall leave his father and mother and be joined to his wife, and the two shall become one'? So they are no longer two but one. What God has joined together, let no man put asunder." Matthew 19:4-6

Now that's rather peculiar addition. When I went to school one plus one equaled two. Jesus is saying that in the profound event of marriage, one plus one still equals one.

Of course there are different ways of looking at this mystery. One man said, "When the preacher told us on our wedding day that we two would become one, my bride had already decided which one."

Or, as one wife said to a friend, "It's so neat, my husband and I like the same things. Of course, it took him twenty years to learn!"

That's not exactly what Jesus had in mind. Let's look at it.

Our Lord said two persons become one. In other words, although you are two distinct individuals, your lives are blended into one entity. We've even got a name for it. You are now a couple. A couple. It has a nice ring to it, doesn't it? Instead of being single, you are a married couple. Your two pasts become one present. Shared responsibility is fashioned out of individual freedoms. Individual goals are now mutual dreams. There are lots of ways in which two are transformed into one.

Jesus said that a man leaves his parents (of course the

woman does, too), so two homes are left and a new home is established. In other words, out of two family trees a new sapling is planted. Each home creates new traditions out of old memories.

In a few minutes, in the Name of God, you will become husband and wife. Your two names will become one. That is important, for names are symbols, and to share the same name illustrates to the world, in a concrete way, the unity of marriage.

Your union as husband and wife was designed by God to be permanent. In no sense should marriage ever be looked upon as experimental or temporary. Jesus was very clear in stating that no one should ever try to divide a husband and wife. What God joins together, no one must separate.

The fact that God creates *one from two* in marriage may sound very romantic, and let me assure you it most certainly is. But times will come when you rebel against this unity. There will be days when each of you may wonder what you saw in the other and you will speak words of disappointment and anger. You may even intentionally hurt each other and may think you would be better off alone. But you are one — you belong together.

Sometimes our wills become so hardened we do not remember that. So it is important for us to worship together and share the good news of Jesus. Through prayer, the healing power of God can penetrate our wills so he can empower us to work out our problems, to overcome our trials, and to experience his comforting presence in our pain. With our Lord's help, a marriage can grow stronger and love can become deeper. We can enjoy the oneness we share in the marriage bond.

The gifts of married life are precious indeed. One oft-used quote substantiates this: "Sharing with another multiplies your joys and divides your sorrows." That is especially true in marriage. When something good happens to us we want to let it out; we have to share it. To have someone who gets excited for you and with you is truly wonderful; it increases your joy. Similarly, when we are disappointed and sadness envelops us, it is good to have someone, someone who cares for us above all others, who will embrace us and give us the assurance of their affection and faithfulness. To have someone stand by you, when a marathon hurt pays a visit, is a great gift.

So it is, _____ and _____, your lives are now so intertwined that you two are one. Whatever happens to one, the repercussions will be felt by the other. Plan on practicing sensitivity to each other. Support and encourage each other. Let your affection show in deed as well as word. Work for the happiness of the other, and your life together will be richer and more fulfilling, because you two are one.

Finally, in the mystery of marriage, as you foster love for each other, your love for God can be increased. I encourage you to worship him and serve him, as with one voice, one life. That will bring a wonderful warmth to your relationship, as Christ brings his divine love to enhance your earthly love. Therein lies joy and happiness in marriage beyond all your hopes and expectations. Amen

Love as Grace

___(Name)___ and __(name)__, you have come to this day and to this place to receive the benediction of Christ upon your union as husband and wife. It's a wonderful place to start.

Today, when everything is so lovely, it seems as if you could be like the prince and the princess who ride off together on a white charger to a honeymoon that lasts forever. Of course, that is only a romantic dream. But then, romantic dreams are the stuff that weddings are made of.

Your marriage, however, must be lived out in down-to-earth ways. And because the emotions of courtship are so explosive and heady, it can be startling to wake up one morning to the realization that marriage is not just hugging and kissing and all that, but is also, pressures, responsibilities, cares, and anxieties. The romantic dreams harbored in your hearts can be cruelly shattered by the harsh realities of life.

That is not to say that the consuming emotional feelings which are the content of courtship are bad; we just can't expect them to last forever. In fact, we could not exist happily for long periods of time with that kind of emotional overload. So I must tell you, _____ and _____, that the wonderful romantic love which envelops you today will fade. But we pray that a much more glorious, mature love will fill its space. Not that you should ever lose the romantic love of courtship; it is a necessary and exciting part of marriage and, in fact, should be fostered. Playfulness in marriage is a delightful way of maintaining a sparkle in your eyes. But a marvelous joy and peace are created when God's kind of love is born into your relationship. I'm talking about grace.

Grace is described as a love which is given without being deserved or earned; it is love which is shared with no strings attached and with no conditions. It asks nothing in return. It is love which just *loves.*

Now that kind of love may seem a bit far-fetched. Our society has primed us to be on the lookout for Number One and to use people for our own ends. That is why mature love (the love defined as grace) must always begin with God. As the Bible says, "We love, because he first loved us." 1 John 4:19

Grace begins with the awareness that God reached out to love you first, and that he loves you "more dearly than the spoken word can say." Because his love for each of you is boundless, he wants you to be extravagant in your love for each other. That's one concrete way his love finds its way into your life. Let me illustrate.

A new Christian came to her pastor telling him of the wonderful new life she had received from Christ. "If only," she exclaimed, "if only I could feel the touch of his hand on me."

"Have you ever prayed for that?" asked the pastor.

When the woman responded with, "No, I never thought of that," the pastor urged her to do it. So, shutting her eyes she prayed, "Please, Lord, lay your hand on me." And as she sat there, suddenly she cried out, "He touched me! He did. I felt his hand on my head." But then, after a moment of reflection she added, "But I really think it was your hand, Pastor."

"Of course it was mine," said the pastor. "Whose hand did you think it would be?"

When God wants to show his love to you, _____, whose hand do you think it will be? And, _____, when God wants to bless you with love, whose hand do you think he will use? In the economy of God, when he wants a hand to touch the life of someone with grace, he usually uses the hand that is nearest. This means that through marriage, you are now special agents of God's grace. You are, as Martin Luther put it, to be "little Christs" to one another.

That's why I can say I hope you love each other *less* today than in any other day of your life. My prayer is that you will grow in grace, unwrapping the grandeur of its meaning as you become, more and more, instruments through which God can bless and strengthen and love you both.

So, _____ and _____, you are joined together by God on this day that you might love each other because he first loved you. May the radiance of your love so warm the world around you that your marriage brings a glory, not only to you but to all the lives you touch. And in all your days, may you find and enjoy God's grace, a love which is deeper and warmer and more wonderful than any you can now anticipate. Amen

The Love which Makes a Marriage

(Name) and (name), as you stand here today I suppose there is nothing more important to you than the love you bear toward each other. After all, isn't that what all the romantic songs tell us? One old standard suggests that love and marriage go together like a horse and carriage. But what is the relationship of a horse to a carriage? And what does that say about the union of two persons?

Or how about the old song, "Love is a Many-Splendored Thing"? That sounds wonderfully romantic. But what kind of love is many-splendored? Self-love? Sexual love? Puppy love? Mother love? You see, a lot depends upon what you mean by love.

Consider the popular song, "Love is the Answer." The answer to what? Our boredom? Our fears? Our hopes and dreams? Our need for acceptance? Our selfishness? And what happens if we discover that love requires sacrifice, that it asks us to give in or give up something — something important like a long-held idea or a lifelong dream? Yes, what happens when love is the question?

I recall the story of a harried wife who arrived at work looking more than a little disheveled. A fellow employee asked, "Did you wake up grumpy this morning?"

Replied the wife, "No, I let him sleep."

If suddenly one or both of you awaken one morning to realize that marriage is not all you dreamed it would be, then what kind of love is the answer?

Many people have been in love just as you are, _____ and _____, and they had high hopes for their marriage. But something happened along the way to erode their love, or to undermine whatever feelings they had for each other.

Part of the problem is we are confused about this matter of love. Through the media we are presented with love which is largely romantic, or sexual, or emotional, as though these kinds of love could form the basis of an enduring relationship.

For instance, romantic love seems exciting and exhilarating. We dream about it, fantasize over it, but really that's all it is — a mental fixation, a frame of mind. It is a love which doesn't think about sweat, and struggle, and dirty dishes, and diapers, and disagreements. Romantic love is really a figment of our imagination and, therefore, it will lead ultimately to disappointment.

Sexual love is powerful and wildly beautiful, but it is tied so tightly to self-love that it really cannot form the foundation for a solid, lovely marriage. When wills clash and troubles erupt, sexual love is too unstable to sustain the relationship and the marriage crumbles.

Emotional love is very important, but emotions are so fickle they cannot be relied upon as the basis of a relationship. Thus, when the chips are down and our relationship is strained, emotional love is found wanting. In fact, it is probably the emotional part of us which first entertains the thought of ending our marriage when the going gets rough.

So it isn't passion which goes together with marriage like a horse and carriage, and emotional infatuation isn't a many-splendored thing, and romantic love is not the answer. What then? What value is love in a marriage if it has no adhesive power to hold a couple together?

Well, I want to assure you, _____ and _____, that love is essential to a lifelong marriage. All the varieties of love I have described are helpful and good, or else God, in his wisdom, would not have made them a part of us. And, I hope you enjoy them all in your relationship. But there is one kind of love which makes marriage an exciting, fulfilling adventure; a love which is stronger and deeper than all the others.

This love has as its source the grace of God in Christ Jesus. Christ's love is the catalyst which makes all the other loves more possible, more wonderful, and more durable. That is not simply church jargon. It is a wonderful reality, which only those who surrender their lives to him can experience.

And what is this love of Christ? What does it entail? It is portrayed for us by St. Paul in the inspired words of 1 Corinthians 13. I recommend to you, _____ and _____, this kind of love to nurture in your marriage. Listen closely as Paul speaks: "Love is patient and kind; love is not jealous, or conceited, or proud; love is not ill-mannered, or selfish, or irritable; love does not keep a record of wrongs; love is not happy with evil, but is happy with the truth. Love never gives up: its faith, hope, and patience never fail." (Good News Bible)

This kind of love endures forever because it creates the basis for an affectionate and secure relationship. I pray that Christ's love will make of your marriage one of great beauty, one which lasts a lifetime. Amen

A Need for Newness

(Name) and _(name)_, in the soft, romantic glow of this candlelight wedding, everything seems so warm and wonderful that it's hard to imagine that you will experience anything in your life except joy and happiness. Everything about your marriage has a newness and a freshness to it. It is so enchanting that you might think you're dreaming.

Of course you're not, although I know you _do_ have dreams — dreams for yourselves as you begin this marvelous enterprise of life. If only you could live the rest of your years with the guarantee that all your days would pass by in peace and happiness as you pursue your dreams of wedded love.

Well, I'm pleased to tell you that it's possible, if you're well-informed. All you need to do is select the right kind of coffee; be sure you know if _____ prefers Stovetop Stuffing over mashed potatoes; keep a plentiful supply of Coke on hand (for Coke adds life); and buy pre-cooked sausages so you won't have to wait for breakfast. Already, if you've been paying attention, you're on your way to marital success, at least according to Madison Avenue.

There's more. If your tensions rise, Compoze will handle the problem; pain is no trouble as long as there's extra-strength Excedrin; and rest assured, Sominex guarantees 100% safe sleep. Furthermore, you will always and forever be fascinated with each other. All you need to do is use Scope (it even smells good); apply the proper deodorant, and sprinkle yourselves liberally with an irresistible after-shave or cologne. Follow these instructions and you will be enchanted with each other — forever!

You are both mature enough to realize that happiness and fulfillment in marriage is far more evasive than that. Yet it is interesting that people buy certain items in the sometimes desperate hope that maybe — just possibly — this or that product can help their relationship, or at least provide a moment of contentment or satisfaction in their marriage. That's a sad fact of life.

The problem is that marriage relationships can easily grow stale. Bored spouses look for something which might rekindle the spark of excitement they once knew. Thus, keeping a marriage fresh is very important. That is why I would share with you a few words from the prophet Jeremiah: "But this I call to mind, and therefore I have hope: The steadfast love of the Lord never ceases, his mercies never come to an end; they are new every morning." Lamentations 3:21-23

The prophet is simply pointing out that God works at keeping our relationship with him alive and vital by pouring out his mercies (his gifts) upon us anew each day. A key to joy in your marriage, _____ and _____, is to follow the example God sets for you.

First you must fasten yourselves to Jesus Christ, for if you worship our Lord *together* and pray to him *for each other*, the cohesive power of the Holy Spirit can enter your lives in beautiful and powerful ways.

Then you must stand ready to forgive each other as Christ yearns to forgive you. Forgiveness brings continual resurrection to a marriage relationship. I tell you sincerely, _____ and _____, that some of the most precious moments of your marriage will be found in times of reconciliation because it is there that love has had to go the deepest and, therefore, finds its greatest expression.

Another way to keep your marriage renewed is to be unsparing in words of love, trust, and encouragement. It is more than sad when couples do not express their affection for each other; nothing can cause a marriage to grow flat faster. Again, we follow the example of our God who is constant in reminding us of his great and steadfast love. Words of encouragement can bring fresh luster to a relationship and, of course, the little phrase, "I love you," when spoken from the heart, never loses its power to revitalize a marriage.

Actions which say, "I love you," are equally important in keeping the romance in marriage akindle. If you continually look for ways to make each other happy, you will always have something to look forward to in life. Each day can bring the possibility of some new experience of joy.

You see, _____ and _____, marriages need to be kept fresh and alive and vital, and it must be done each day — every day. Marriage cannot be preserved against the future; it has to be won fresh each new day.

So today you begin one of life's great experiences, the relationship of marriage. It can be a source of great joy and satisfaction for you both. I pray that you will live in close harmony with our Lord Jesus Christ. Through your fellowship with him, God can constantly flood you with the gifts of love, patience, kindness, and unselfishness. And, like his mercies, your love will never come to an end; it will be renewed every morning. Amen

How God Blesses a Marriage

__(Name)__ and __(name)__, it is good that you are here, in this church, with relatives and friends, to take your holy vows and to begin your life as husband and wife. What a great day of celebration! Most importantly, our Lord is here to accept you both and to bless you, through his presence, and through you to each other. The opportunities of sharing the love of Christ are greater in marriage than in any other relationship. Thus we cherish for you, _____, that God has chosen you to be an instrument of his mercy; through you he will show His love to _____ in a very special way. And we are glad for you, _____, that the radiance of God's love will be demonstrated in a unique way through you to _____.

It's very precious, this love which God bestows on us. But its true glory lies in the fact that we do not have to earn it, or work for it, or trade for it. It is simply given to us — no strings attached! This is the kind of love which God would have us reflect toward each other in marriage. It is a love that demands no response, a love that gives without thought of return, a love which seeks only the joy of the beloved. It is grace. Grace is, at once, the most powerful and the least powerful ingredient in a joy-filled marriage. It is powerful because it is the only power that can conquer the human heart, that almost impregnable fortress. And grace is powerless because it can do nothing except by consent. Grace never overpowers.

The psalmist illustrated this winsome truth when he wrote: "Unless the Lord builds the house, those who build it labor in vain. Unless the Lord watches over the city, the watchman stays awake in vain. It is in vain that you rise up early and go late to rest, eating the bread of anxious toil; for he (God) gives to his beloved sleep." Psalm 127:1-2

While that is a description of our dependence on God, it is even more an illustration of grace. Most things in life require that we work hard for them; we get things the old-fashioned way. "We earn them." After all, we live in a "you get what you deserve" kind of world. Whether you are a nurse or a pastor, a student or farmer, or anything else, you must labor faithfully, do your best to deserve your position and receive your pay. But the psalmist warns that all you are searching for and amassing in this world can be futile unless the Lord adds the dimension and meaning and nourishment that only he can.

It goes even deeper than that. The words, "he gives to his beloved sleep," indicate that God's blessings, his gifts, have nothing to do with success or status or the attainment of things in this world. The psalmist is telling us that the content and meaning of life, including the rewards of marriage, do not come from the sweat of our brow or from the things for which we work so hard. They come as we relax in the knowledge of God's great love for us and share his love with each other. Indeed, God's most glorious gifts often come when we least expect them, in areas we would never have guessed, at a time when they are most needed.

What it means is this: the avenues of joy will be hidden from our eyes as long as we focus only on this harried and busy world, as long as our energies are spent in anxiety, fear, and frustration. It is only as we are content to rest in the knowledge that all things work together for good to those who love God, and cast all things on him — our fears, our cares, our work, our relationships — that he can free us to enjoy the beauty of his grace which is able to refresh our marriage, our outlook, indeed, our very lives. Jesus put it another way when he said we are to consider first the kingdom of God; then the joy, peace, contentment, and harmony which we need, will be ours as well.

God gives to his beloved in sleep. What a lovely truth. God's gifts are unmerited, unearned, undeserved, treasures of grace, but they are the real joys of life. In your marriage, too, grace must abound. Indeed, your lives should mirror the same unselfish love which God showers upon you. The soft flow of a blessed marriage does not come from trying to deserve or earn the love and favor of each other, because we, too, "give to our beloved in sleep." You are to rest in your relationship and simply give of yourselves so that your marriage might be all God wants it to be.

However, the greatest joy is not in receiving grace, but in giving it. The nature of love is that the more you give, the more you receive. Love cannot be hoarded; it can only be shared. As the old song said so simply, "A song is not a song until you sing it. A bell is not a bell until you ring it. And love was not put in your heart to stay. For love isn't love until you give it away."

_____ and _____, our prayers go with you as you leave this service to begin your labor of love together. Hold fast to this: unless Christ builds your home with you, you labor in vain. It is useless to rise early and go late to rest, just to attain a certain standard of living or reach a certain goal. For then life merely becomes an obstacle course — a merry-go-round — as you eat, and toil, and live out a worry-fraught existence. But live in — and generously share with each other — the grace of God, for he promises thereby to bring joy into your marriage, through each other, in unique and mystifying ways. May you discover the blessing of God in your years together. Amen

Grounds for Marriage

   (Name) and   (name) , this ceremony marks the culmination of your courtship. If you are like most lovers, the road of romance was filled with doubts and hopes, with problems and disappointments, with moments of heart swelling joy and the wonder of blossoming love. Now you have come boldly to declare that love before God and your invited guests. We are thrilled to share these moments with you.

It would be nice to be unreservedly optimistic about your future. But I can't, because marriage isn't a one-way ride on the happiness express. An example of what can happen is illustrated by a story I once heard. A dog-tired business man came home from the office only to hear his wife announce that the cook had quit.

"Why?" he asked.

"Because of you," she fired back.

"Me? What did I do?"

"Well," the wife said, "the cook claimed you called on the phone this afternoon, that you used coarse and abusive language, and you insulted her womanhood."

"Oh no," the man responded, "that's too bad. I thought I was talking to you."

It happens. It happens if we stop courting each other and cherishing each other once the wedding ceremony is over. That is why I want you to listen closely as I share some profound and helpful words from St. Paul: "[I pray] that according to the riches of his glory, [God] may grant you to be strengthened with might through his Spirit in the inner man, and that Christ may dwell in your hearts through faith; that you, being rooted and grounded in love, may have power to comprehend with all the saints what is the breadth and length and height and depth, and to know the love of Christ which surpasses knowledge, that you may be filled with all the fulness of God." Ephesians 3:16-19

That passage is packed with power, but I would like to concentrate on the words, "Being rooted and grounded in love."

_____ and _____, the odds of your having a happy marriage are not, unfortunately, very high. Statistics tell us that only about twenty-two percent of married couples report they have found happiness. But your chances take a quantum leap forward if your relationship is rooted and grounded in love. Now that may seem like an obvious thing to say to a young couple who are madly in love and who are about to express their devotion for a lifetime. After all, who is more in love than a bride and groom?

There is strong evidence that brides and grooms have not yet experienced the depths of love because they are still overwhelmed by infatuation. True love is more than being emotionally, mentally, and physically involved with a person; it is incredibly more profound than passion. That is why a relationship which does not grow beyond physical attraction, never becomes rooted and grounded in love, and eventually crumbles.

Countless marriages have failed simply because the persons never fell in love. I shouldn't say "fell in love" as though it is something you stumble into. Actually, we *grow in love*. I want to emphasize that you have not on this day accomplished one of the great goals of life. You have merely established the direction your lives are taking. You are joining forces to run the gamut of life together and to do it within the context of a new family. But the love which you feel at this moment needs to mature and deepen. I say again, this love is not an emotion, for feelings can be momentary; they fluctuate at a moment's notice; they rise and fall, flash and fade. Love is not an emotion because you cannot be *in* love one day and *out* of love the next. True love has an enduring quality; it is like a rock. That is why love is something you can build a life upon. To use a crude analogy, love is a lot like concrete. The substance is at first very warm and soft, and easily disturbed. However, as time passes the concrete solidifies until it is strong enough to become a foundation capable of supporting great buildings. Real love is like that. It creates a foundation of security. It becomes a firm ground upon which you can walk confidently all your days.

What is the love in which you are to be rooted and grounded? It is the same kind of love God illustrated for us in the life of Jesus. That is why Paul so desires that we get to know the love of Christ. However, we can't read books on it because it surpasses knowledge; it has to be experienced.

There are characteristics of Christ's love — telltale signs of its existence. His love is patient and kind, when every fibre of our being wants to fly off the handle and hurt someone. Christ's love is not jealous, even when our insecurities want to enslave another to us. This kind of love is not rude, even if we know each other so well we can *get by* with coarse language and lack of manners. And listen to this: Christian love does not insist on its own way, even when we believe our way is the best way. Love is not irritable, even though everything seems to be going wrong. It bears all things, believes all things, hopes all things, endures all things.

It is obvious, _____ and _____, that Christ's kind of love will take time to develop, but it should be the goal of your marriage; for being rooted and grounded in that kind of love can bring you joy and fulfillment. Of course it doesn't happen overnight. That kind of love is only born today. It must grow from this day onward. That is why you will need to come to God in prayer daily, that you might be given the strength to live in this love and be endowed with the grace to forgive when you fail.

I repeat Paul's great words in the hope that they follow you throughout your lives and that you make them your own:

"I pray, [_____ and _____], that you may have your roots and foundations in love, so that you, together with all God's people, may have the power to understand how broad and long, and how high and deep, is Christ's love. Yes, may you come to know his love — although it can never be fully known — and to be completely filled with the very nature of God." (Good News Bible) Amen

The Foundation of Faithfulness

(Name) and _(name)_, on this your wedding day I am reminded of a phrase that has appeared on many posters and even some bumper stickers. It is this: "This is the first day of the rest of your lives."

It is, you know. Everything you have done, even when you did it together, you did as two individuals. From this day forward, things will be different. For God has ordained that on this day, through your vows, he will bind you together in a mysterious but wonderful union. So you are no longer two, but one. That makes today the first day of the rest of your lives.

All this may sound exciting to newlyweds, but apparently it is shortlived. That we rebel against the unity of marriage is obvious from the demeaning way in which we speak of it. For instance, one old French adage offers: "Love is the dawn of marriage, and marriage is the sunset of love." It sounds as though love creates the grounds for marriage, but marriage cannot sustain love.

I tell you that just the opposite is true. Love does not make marriage possible; marriage makes love possible. It's true. Just think about it for a while. Deep, responsive love is possible only when the element of faithfulness is present. You can love someone as friend only when trust is present, when you know you can rely on them. The serious love of a relationship begins to blossom when you find someone who accepts you as you are, and who stands by you always. Love is built on faithfulness. You don't need faithfulness for infatuation, or sex, or romance. But marital love is created in faithfulness. That is why the commitment of marriage makes glorious, deep, abiding love possible.

Now in saying this I am not suggesting that romance and sexuality are not important. They are. They are vital and exciting elements of a happy, fulfilling marriage. But there really *is* no marriage if love, the love created out of fidelity, is not present.

So I encourage you, _____ and _____, to take more seriously than ever before this whole matter of absolute commitment to each other. I'm not just talking about faithfulness to each other in sexual matters. I'm speaking about being true to each other in *every* area of life. The more completely we are able to trust one another, the deeper and more wonderful our love grows. To be able to trust another implicitly, is a thing of great wonder. In that security, love takes on marvelous dimensions.

We are not talking about something new. This kind of faithfulness has been a part of our lives for as long as we can remember. The psalmists, for instance, saw faithfulness as a most remarkable and wonderful feature of God. Listen to this song of praise: "O give thanks to the Lord, for he is good, for his steadfast love endures for ever. O give thanks to the God of gods, for his steadfast love endures for ever. O give thanks to the Lord of lords, for his steadfast love endures for ever." Psalm 136:1-3 Our love, at its best, imitates God's love — strong and steadfast.

There's a story which illustrates what I've been trying to say. We all recall the famous ship, Titanic, and how it sank, killing hundreds of people. Among the people aboard the Titanic were a Mr. and Mrs. Isidor Straus. When it became obvious that the ship was going down, Mr. Straus tried everything he could think of to persuade his wife to leave the sinking ship and join the other women and children in the lifeboats. But, to his words, Mrs. Straus replied, "Isidor, you and I will remain together. I will be faithful to you, even if it means death." And so it happened. They died together, faithful unto death.

It's a moving story of love and devotion. But that's the way it is. Love and faithfulness go hand-in-hand, creating beauty in marriage and wonder in life, even unto death.

That kind of stalwart faithfulness, and that heartwarming shape of love are possible for you, _____ and _____. But to experience it, you will need to grow in strength, courage, and faith. God, however, is willing and eager to come to your aid, and God is faithful; his steadfast love endures forever. He has promised never to leave you nor forsake you. He has promised that if you confess your sins, he will forgive your sins. He has promised to give you strength for every situation you face in life. You can trust God. He who spared not his own Son, but gave him up for us all, is absolutely reliable.

That is why I urge you, as husband and wife, to be faithful in your spiritual lives as well, to nurture the gift of faith God has given you. In constantly re-experiencing the faithfulness of God, and living in the assurance of his mercy and grace, you can confidently live out your lives before him. His presence will supply you with the power to live in ways that are pleasing to him, and eternally fulfilling for yourselves. He has promised his faithfulness so that, through his Spirit, he might strengthen you to be faithful to each other, that your love might grow in beauty and depth.

_____ and _____, as your family and friends, we want to find happiness and joy in each other, that you may be able to celebrate all the wonders of life which God places be-fore you. Our prayers will follow you as you leave this place that, in faithfulness to each other, you may discover the glories of love which God intends that you should know and experience. Truly this is the first day of the rest of your lives. Amen

44

An Offer from God

___(Name)___ and ___(name)___, you haven't exactly had what would be called a whirlwind romance. Now all those years of courtship and months and months of preparation are being distilled into these brief but precious moments, which comprise your wedding day.

What do you say to a young couple who are deeply in love but who are still largely innocent of the demands of love? What do you say to two dear young people who know the joy of a close relationship, but who have yet to deal with the frictions which the intimacy of marriage brings? I know you want, more than anything else, to have a happy marriage. That's the way it should be. But how will the future deal with you? And how could any words help you cope with all the possibilities for good or ill?

I could give you some good advice, like "Keep the tender art of romance alive in your marriage by constantly saying, 'I love you,' in word and deed. And, keep the bridges of communication in good working order by taking the time to explore the depth of each other's personality. And, be sure to mature together, not only by developing a hearty sense of humor, but also by developing mutual interests."

All that *is* sound advice, and if you want a meaningful life, you would be wise to follow it. But there is something more I hold before you today, and that is the offer God makes to you on this your wedding day. An offer. You can take it or leave it. But if you are sincere about wanting a warm, growing, and wonderful marriage, it is an offer too good to pass up. God's offer is simply this: he will give you all you really need if you give yourselves to him. St. Paul put it this way, ". . . but [Christ] said to me, 'My grace is sufficient for you . . .' " 2 Corinthians 12:9a

Paul was most likely referring to his health problems, but his words ring true regardless of what problems we have. For Christians are not spared the difficulties of life. Jesus himself endured great adversity. But Paul assures us that, as we encounter the joys and trials of life, we can have at our disposal a power far greater than our own. From my own experience I can attest to the fact that God is able to reach into our lives in very special ways through the gift of faith. Nowhere is this more true than in a marriage relationship. If our marriages are offered to God, it increases the chance that our relationship will become a blessing rather than an endurance contest.

There are some good reasons for this. First, forgiveness is more apt to be practiced. In worship we are continually reminded of God's grace, his undeserved love. He is always ready to forgive us, so we are urged to pardon each other. Grace always seeks reconciliation. Always. Beyond that, the Christian view of marriage stresses our oneness. We (husband and wife) are one. Therefore, no blunder, no harsh word, no sin, is entirely one person's fault. If we are really "one flesh," then shouldn't both share the blame of the wrong-doing? And if we recognize our shared responsibility, then forgiveness becomes more possible. The beautiful thing about forgiveness, if it is like God's forgiving grace, is that whatever stood between the spouses is gone. The marriage will not just be *patched up,* it will begin anew, on a stronger, firmer basis.

Second, the grace of God in Christ is a tremendous source of strength. We cannot see into the future, but we know that misfortune and difficulties are commonplace in any marriage. With Christ's grace active in our lives, we are able to lean on him and his ever-present power. In other words, our Lord goes with us on the adventure of marriage. His grace sustains us. It allows us to say with Christians over the years, "I do not know what the future holds, but I know who holds the future."

Third, Christ's grace is sufficient to overcome selfishness. There is perhaps, no greater problem in a marriage than self-centeredness. That is, no doubt, because from childhood we have been trained to take care of ourselves first. But Jesus tells us that we are to look for his appearance in the people we meet in our everyday lives. This means that whatever you _____ do for _____, you do also for Jesus. And whatever you, _____ do, for _____, is like doing it for your Lord. Faith permits you to see Christ in each other. There is no greater motivation for treating each other with kindness and respect than that. It is our acts of charity, with no thought of response, which give us our greatest joy and fill our hearts with the greatest pleasure.

Finally, _____ and _____, Christ's grace enhances the love you bear for each other. As you come to love your Lord more, your love for each other will be enriched. God gives us eyes to see each other through the eyes of faith, and our love is nourished and increased through his love. That is one of the wonderful surprises of a life in Christ.

So, as family and friends, we urge you to accept the offer God makes to you today. In so doing, may he bless your marriage and the love you share each day of your life. Amen

The Crisis of Marriage

__(Name)__ and __(name)__ , I rejoice with you today, and I know your families are pleased, too — glad that you are making this leap of faith into marriage. Life has not been easy on either of you, but you have come today to publicly make a statement of hope and optimism because of your mutual love. It's exciting, not only for you, but for us all.

This event is going to create some jarring changes in your lives, and you will experience more than a little stress. You might even call it a crisis. Now I know we usually associate the word *crisis* with something negative, but that's not necessarily the case. Any event which creates tension, for good or bad, is called a crisis.

In the past you have both experienced some tragic crises, and you carry scars because of them. Those scars, however, are signs of victory. Although they remind you sadly of your pain, they have healed over to signal you have won. You cannot deny those painful and sometimes nostalgic memories, yet you now courageously step forward, willing to commit yourselves in love, in spite of it all.

You, of all people, know that life is not a walk down some glib and giddy path. It is filled with work and worry, happiness and heartache, loveliness and loneliness. Yet today you cast your lot to walk that path *together*. You will face your sorrows and your joys — *together*. You will meet the successes of life, along with its frustrations and failures — together. It's a beautiful word: *together*. It means you no longer need to be alone. In all the circumstances of life you will have *each other* and your loved ones, with their support and encouragement. Today may be a crisis, a life-changing event, but not in a negative way at all. It can be an opportunity for a wonderful adventure.

Furthermore, you share the blessings of God. As you worship together, pray together, and share your faith and affection, God works to make your lives more beautiful, enabling your love to grow deeper, stronger, and more sturdy. Giving God a primary place in your marriage can only serve to make you more secure, for you will be embraced by his everlasting arms and his grace will be sufficient for all your needs.

It's true. Consider the picture Paul used in the passage you selected from Colossians: ". . . let the peace of Christ rule in your hearts." Colossians 3:15 The word *rule* is a verb used in athletics, and describes the activity of the umpire or referee; he settles things. Paul is saying that we are to let God's peace decide things in our lives, or, literally, "Let the peace of Christ be the referee in your marriage." Since Christ loves you both so deeply, you can be sure his peace will move you in the way of understanding, love, and harmony. It is a wonderful thing to have God on your side, enriching your relationship!

So, _____ and _____, you are now committing yourselves to each other "to become one, sharing God's love." As family and friends, who love you and care for you, we pray that God will supply you with all you need as you face this glorious crisis called marriage. May our Lord bless you and bring fulfillment to you, through each other, for the rest of your lives. Amen

The Bondage of Marriage

(Name) and _(name)_, if you were like 99.99% of engaged couples contemplating their wedding day, it was exciting. But in the future, as you look back, you might find yourself asking _why_ you looked forward to this moment. You might agree with the poet Keats, who suggested in his ode (poem), "On a Grecian Urn," that anticipation provides greater enjoyment than participation. The truth is, many look back on their wedding day with feelings which range all the way from wistful nostalgia to bitter cynicism and grief.

You see, the romantic dreams of marriage don't last long; what your heart desires and what your marriage becomes may be miles apart. As evidence, consider the way people talk about marriage. Some women complain that they are home-bound or are "unpaid maids." Some men speak of being "chained in" or "whipped into shape" by their wives. Interesting isn't it, how words suggesting servanthood and slavery creep into our descriptions of marriage?

But perhaps it isn't so strange. After all, listen to what Paul says about marriage: "Be subject to one another out of reverence for Christ." Ephesians 5:21

Let's look at those words in the context of Jesus' commandment: "What therefore God has joined together let no man put asunder." Mark 10:9 The Greek word translated, "joined together," carries the meaning of being fused together, welded into one unit. In other words, God does not join a couple simply to go through life side by side as a mere mating of individuals. He says that through marriage the two persons become a new creation. God bonds the two personalities together in a dynamic way so they cannot be separated without painful and irreparable damage to both. So, we could say that, in one sense, marriage is indeed a bondage.

However, the bondage of marriage is not one of coercion, a bondage of power. In no way is marriage like slavery. It is servanthood by choice, in a self-imposed bondage of love. We choose to marry because we want to commit our heart and our life to another. Willingly, joyfully we make our sacred vows, in order that we may be subject to one another out of reverence for Christ, yes, but also for the sake of love.

Now this idea runs counter to current pop psychology which encourages men and women to assert their independence. The special relationship of wife and husband is seen in terms of self-serving rather than in self-sacrifice. Marriage is viewed as a vehicle to achieve personal objectives rather than as a means to pursue mutual goals.

That is why what I say to you may not be very popular in some circles, but it is Christian.

Paul says that in marriage you are to be subject to one another, so you can no longer say, "It's my life; I can do with it as I please." In whatever one does, the other is mysteriously involved. That means marriage is not a fifty-fifty proposition. We humans are exceedingly poor in determining percentages. Rather, marriage must be a 100-100 proposition, with each partner giving their all, that the relationship might grow in beauty and depth.

This does not mean you will stop being individuals. Even when you are apart, your love will contain the other, support the other, and recall the other. Very romantic. But you see, the concept of submission in marriage is the most romantic of all, for it asks not, "What can I get?" but, more gloriously, "What can I give so we can celebrate our oneness and our love?"

It is natural that our wills rebel against submission, and it is inevitable that you will experience pain and hurt. Fortunately, God comes to offer you his personal help. If you submit yourselves to Christ, he can provide the healing power to bring you back together again. That's why I encourage you to worship together and to pray together. When you are continually warmed by God's love, it will become easier for you to ask him into your relationships to fill you with his amazing grace. Then submission to each other, for Jesus' sake, becomes not a law but a privilege. And by his grace your marriage can be filled with joy, surpassing even your fondest dreams.

So I do not agree with the poet Keat's premise that anticipation is greater and more enjoyable than the realization of an event — at least not when applied to marriage. For although you have enjoyed being with each other and loving each other, you will find that if you submit to one another out of love, your greatest joys and most endearing moments are yet to come. Amen

Creating a Happy Marriage

(Name) and _(name)_, you are wonderfully idealistic and determined to have a happy marriage. And all who are present here are standing in your corner, cheering you on. Truly you are fortunate to have such a loving family and such faithful friends, supporting you during these awesome moments when you make sacred and lifelong promises to each other. We will stand by you as you leave this place as well, because we want you to be happy tomorrow and tomorrow.

However, happiness is not something we find or just stumble upon. It is something which finds us when we create the conditions for it to happen.

An anonymous clergyman put it well: "The trouble is that young people think of marriage as the road to happiness. They expect automatically to alight on happiness as soon as they are married. They expect that love will float them into bliss. The fact is, there is little about marriage in itself to make for happiness, while there are plenty of things about marriage to make for problems. Two personalities waiting to be happy come into a relationship, the most intimate that earth knows, where all the peculiarities of one are thrust on the sensitiveness of the other. That situation by itself is much more likely to make for agony rather than bliss."

That attitude may not sound optimistic, but it is realistic. Even the vows which you are making to each other, whether you realize it or not, acknowledge the same thing; marriage is not instant happiness. Let's look at them.

You first promise to accept each other "for better or worse." Of course your minds have focused on the "better" — and that's good — but because we are sinful human beings, there's a lot of "worse" in marriage as well. You will need to practice forgiving.

Next you vow to accept each other "for richer, for poorer." Of course, we all hope that your lot in life will be richer, rather than poorer. But you know, rarely does any of us think we have enough, and determining what you are going to spend those precious dollars on can put a strain on the best of relationships.

You will need to set goals and plan together. You are pledging also to stay by each other "in sickness and in health." The words are easy to say, but caring for a mate who is seriously ill or who becomes handicapped can be an exhausting experience. We hope you are blessed with good health, but no one gets through life scotfree. You will need to be constant in prayer for each other.

So, _____ and _____, you are already acknowledging that there are possibilities for hurts as well as happiness in marriage. That's why achieving happiness is such an extraordinary blessing. A recent Gallup Poll reported that only twenty percent of all couples interviewed evaluated their marriage as being happy. Only one out of five! How tragic, when we know that every couple begins their life together with the hope of happiness.

Let me say it again. Happiness is not something that just happens to you, as though happy couples are *just lucky*. You can work at creating the atmosphere which makes happiness more possible by living in God's love and sharing that with each other. Then, even in the midst of the betters and worses, the richers or poorers, the sicknesses and healths of life you will have the confidence that God is with you and he will see you through. He will not just see you through, but will also enable you to win the victory, come what may.

I know that is true because the Bible says not once, but repeatedly: God will be with us. Jesus' final words were: ". . . lo, I am with you always." Matthew 28:20 And I remind you that Jesus said he came into this aching, unhappy world for this express purpose: "That you might have life — life in all its fulness." John 10:10 (Good News Bible) In other words, Christ came to bring us fulfillment and joy.

So, if you two, and for that matter, the rest of us, can take the hand of Christ and stride into life with all the possibilities for heartache and "heartsing," then you, and we, can live out life with the presence and the power of God at our disposal. There's a lot of security and joy in that. Holy Marriage is intended to be not only holy, but a lot of fun, and the source of great happiness.

_____ and _____, trust God, love the Lord, and use the opportunity of marriage to do all you can to bring happiness to each other. Then you will know joy. Because happiness cannot be grasped and laid hold of, it must be given to us. May you, therefore, give to each other, and may our loving God give you, *through* each other, happiness beyond your highest hopes. Amen

One Husband's Counsel

___

   (Name) and   (name) , what a marvelous day this is for us. In this moment we have come to stand by you as, in the presence of our Lord, you experience one of the most precious and important events of your life — your wedding. We are here to assure you that because we love you, we will pray for you and support you as you go out from this place. For we know that happy weddings are a dime a dozen; happy marriages are rare.

   Unfortunately, there are no self-help books, no "Ten Steps to Marital Bliss" which can ensure a strong, joyous marriage. But St. Peter in his first letter gives some sound words of wisdom. Peter, you might recall, is the only disciple who we know for sure was married. Listen to his husbandly counsel. ". . . Have unity of spirit, sympathy, love of [each other], a tender heart and a humble mind. Do not return evil for evil or [insult for insult]; but on the contrary bless, for to this you have been called, that you may obtain a blessing." 1 Peter 3:8-9

   Peter, as a husband, knows that a good marriage takes more than determination; it requires selfless love, patience, and self-sacrifice. It also takes an awareness that a married couple is, in fact, a single entity. So he speaks of having unity of spirit.

   It's a fact. Your lives are now so inextricably bound that every action and every word, directly or indirectly, affects the other. You have great power over each other, power to make the other either happy or depressed. But you cannot cause sorrow to your mate without losing something of the dignity and beauty of love in the process, just as you cannot bring happiness without adding to your own enjoyment of life. As you become united in marriage, you hold the emotions of each other in your hands. God grant you the wisdom to hold them gently, with compassion.

Peter also counsels you to have sympathy, and stresses how important this is in a good marriage. To know that someone stands by you no matter how rugged and rough the times become, is a great blessing. One thing is clear: sympathy and selfishness cannot occupy the same space. Sympathy requires that we forget ourselves, step outside ourselves, and identify with the cares and problems of our mate. It is within the arena of sympathy and compassion that love grows deeper and more lovely than any newlyweds can possibly imagine.

Another point of Peter's counsel is to remain humble. Sad is the marriage when one or both of the spouses think they could have done better or feel they got the raw end of the marriage. It can happen. It is very easy to take our mate for granted, to forget virtues, and to concentrate on faults. We are all sinful and imperfect people, who are difficult to live with at times. Never lose the capacity to marvel at the fact that your mate chose to marry you, warts and all!

Then Peter counsels you to be forgiving. Forgiveness is the heart of happiness. We know that hostility upsets our bodies and our lives. To be at odds with one's mate creates an agony which consumes our energy and dominates our thoughts. Strange, then, that we do not seek reconciliation more readily. I assure you, you will save much time and emotional wear and tear by being willing to seek reconciliation. Do not return evil for evil or insult for insult; be mature enough to reach out to each other with forgiveness and love.

Peter concludes his counsel by urging you to be a blessing. The best way this happens is to create a home in which Christ is present. Attending worship together has a cohesive influence on a relationship; devotions together brings some of the most healing interludes of life. Opening our hearts and our home to Christ in no way diminishes our happiness in marriage — far from it — for he brings his blessing and joy and peace whereever he resides. And you know, the more you revel in his blessings, the more of a blessing you will be to each other and to all whose lives are graced by yours.

So then, _____ and _____, we are sending you off with our prayers and our love. In following the counsel of Peter, may you discover all the great and wonderful things that God has planned for your future. As you do, you will truly be a blessing to each other, to your loved ones, and to your God. May he watch over your days and your deeds in his peace. Amen

Together . . . Till Death Us Do Part

(Name) and _(name)_, the word *overwhelming* was made for a day like today. No words will ever be able to describe how you feel. Yet the closeness you feel toward your Lord and toward each other on this day is only the beginning of a lifetime of surprises, and gifts, and joys, God has in store for you. Knowing this, we, your family, relatives, and friends, have gathered to celebrate this momentous and sacred event with you. We are here to assure you of our affection and to under-gird you with our prayers.

In the midst of all the emotions you feel, I would break into your thoughts with some good news from Jesus. Words not only for you, but for all who are present. Words which may not sound appropriate for a wedding, but I believe they fit. They are strong, dynamic words of grace which can revive and strengthen all our relationships. From the Gospel of Mark: "If any man would come after me, let him deny himself and take up his cross and follow me." Mark 8:34

That word from Christ speaks directly, not only to the matter of marriage, but to all of life, for he is speaking about commitment! I am well aware that the popular cry of our generation is one of liberation: "Let me first of all be free!" But the startling truth is that there can be no genuine, fulfilling liberation unless we stand first of all on the bedrock of commitment.

Of course, the liberation movements sound attractive. Often there is the assumption that loving, profound, lifelong relationships are the exception rather than the rule. So we are bombarded with facile verbiage like: "Think of yourself first." "You don't owe anyone anything."

A women's magazine I read some time ago advised women to refuse to sacrifice for the family. The idea was to think of one's self. You come first. You have to grow, too. Let others do the sacrificing. Don't make commitments which cannot be easily broken.

Last year I read a newspaper article which suggested that men think of marriage like they think of a job. Don't plan on staying married to the same person for the whole of your life. You need variety, so think of several marriages for different stages in your life.

The rhetoric of some liberation movements demonstrates a brutal disregard for others, overlooking the possibility of a love which becomes richer and more meaningful as a couple grows together in marriage. But of course, if a relationship is not built on absolute commitment, if there is no one we can trust, then it stands to reason that life becomes a treacherous, anxiety-ridden experience and we develop throw away relationships. You see, we must always be careful that no one makes a fool of us.

What then shall we say to this? Jesus said if anyone wants to become a follower of his, they need to leave self behind; they must take up their cross and come with him. Whoever puts one's self first is lost; but if anyone is willing to live humbly, like a servant, they will find their true self. Jesus is saying that a preoccupation with self can keep us from the real meaning of life. The deepest needs and requirements of our lives cannot be met within ourselves. They must be found in relationships, with God, and with other people. The fruits of love, joy, and peace are the by-products of faithful, lifelong commitment. We need, as husband and wife, to assure each other of our faithfulness, to speak it to each other, and to live it out, so we might experience its wonder and power, together . . . till death us do part.

Our calling is to be a *committed* people. We need commitment, for we cannot live securely in fragile relationships which might break at any time. We cannot be at peace when one partner lays down conditions for acceptance. We cannot celebrate love at its deepest levels if another will not give totally of himself. We need persons we can call on, fall back on, rely on, and rest in. That's why Jesus' invitation to deny ourselves and follow him is not bad news, but good news. For when we put our Lord first, the other things of this world fall into their proper persective. Then things, even valuable things, become dispensable. Blunders in relationships become forgivable; people become reliable. Love becomes possible; and hope can surge in our hearts.

When we have committed our lives to Christ he can free us, liberate us, in the truest sense of the word. Then we can live out our lives to the fullest, enjoying, but not being bound to, all the gifts God gives us. For Jesus' promise was, and is, if a person will surrender their life and lose it in him, they will find their true self.

_____ and _____, our prayer is that in committing your life to God, he will strengthen you to keep the commitments you have made to each other, that you may celebrate being *together* . . . till death you do part. As you are faithful, the lives of many will be blessed through you. Amen

The Beauty of Marriage

__(Name)__ and __(name)__, this is a very special day in your lives. You have gone to great lengths to make it beautiful. Now if only there were some way to insure that your marriage would be beautiful, all the days of your life. I say this, remembering what one wit said, "There's entirely too much worrying about unhappy marriages. Everyone knows that all marriages are happy. It's getting along together *after* the marriage that creates the problems."

I think you would agree that almost every marriage begins beautifully; maintaining beauty in the relationship is infinitely more difficult. However, God has left you neither helpless nor hopeless. He has a great investment in you both, and his promise is that he will stand by you to provide you with his mercies, that your marriage might grow in depth and glory.

St. John writes of how God shares his love with us, but he also suggests how a marriage can develop an enduring quality of loveliness: "In this the love of God was made manifest among us, that God sent his only Son into the world, so that we might live through him. In this is love, not that we loved God, but that he loved us and sent his Son to be the expiation for our sins. Beloved, if God so loved us, we also ought to love one another." 1 John 4:9-11

Telling you, or any bride and groom standing before an altar, that you must love each other sounds as needless as commanding a three-year-old to eat a candy bar. After all, isn't that what marriage is all about — love?

The truth is, the kind of love John speaks of is far different from what people usually mean when they talk of love. Love is most often regarded as a romantic feeling, but for John, love is far deeper, more beautiful, and more consuming. John's love is not an emotion; it is an event. He refers to the kind of love God has for us. When God wanted to reveal his love to us in its most awesome wonder, he permitted his Son, Jesus, to be crucified. In the crucified Christ, God showed us he was willing to go further than anyone could be asked, in order to prove his love. It was on Calvary that God in Christ redefined love for us. God was saying that love is forgiveness; love is reconciliation; love is restoring, healing, helping: therein is love!

And so, _____ and _____, when John tells you to love one another, he is not saying something that is patently obvious. In reality he is saying nothing less than this: you are both dearly loved by God. Now he has given each of you the responsibility of bearing that sacrificial kind of love into your relationship. In other words, God's love and grace take human form as you care for and share with each other. That means the love you are to foster in your marriage is not simply a feeling, no matter how warm and affectionate, but an action. God's kind of love is always at work. It is not so much a noun as it is a verb. It is a love which works toward harmony and fulfillment. It is a love which grows out of the emotions of courtship to create charitable acts of compassion and kindness.

_____ and _____, love will be evident in your marriage when you forgive one another. Love will be illustrated when there is healing and encouragement. Love will be practiced when you help each other and support one another. A love that works to help, heal, restore, and forgive, can make your marriage beautiful — exquisitely beautiful — not only for yourselves, but for all who are in your company.

Love is an event first demonstrated for us by our Lord who gave himself for us. Now he invites you, _____ and _____, to continue that self-giving love in your married life. It will not always be easy. The love which is in the shape of forgiveness will need to be practiced often; there is no other way for you to be truly happy.

And remember, the God who created the institution of marriage is as near as your thoughts. Through devotions, prayers, and regular worship he can constantly remind you of his burning love. Through the Holy Spirit he can give you the mind of Christ, which will soften your wills so God's kind of selfsacrificing love can become active in your lives. For only the love which is an event — the love that heals, forgives, strengthens, and restores — abides forever. Love which is active can make your marriage a thing of beauty from beginning to end.

We celebrate this day, this day of love, for today you are brought together and united in an atmosphere of charm and beauty. Our prayers will follow you, that living in God's glorious grace, and you may find your marriage growing in beauty as the years pass by. Amen

Title

Since we've had an opportunity to talk together over the past few months, _(Name)_ and _(name)_, you might think I would soon run out of words of advice. You should know by now that this is one thing parents have in unlimited quantity!

Yet what I'm going to say is not really advice; a hope you will see it (or should I say *hear* it) as good news.

We all remember the fairy tales in which the prince married the beautiful princess. After the ceremony, they rode off to his castle to "live happily ever after." Many of the modern romances in books and movies are described and pictured until the day after the wedding. Then, we are to assume, the couple lives forever in a state of wedded bliss.

You are both mature and wise enough to know that everlasting ecstasy does not follow on the heels of the wedding. Yet harbored deep within the heart of every bride and groom is the idea, the hope, that perhaps their marriage will be the perfect marriage — that the dissension and discord which intrude upon so many marriages will not contaminate their own. And if problems do arise, they will be very minor and infreqent. That's a good wish to have.

But wishing does not accomplish anything. In order to bring any wish to fulfillment one must work to bring it about. The same is true of marriage. A healthy, happy marriage cannot be built on wishes. It is not an accident. It doesn't just happen. When you observe a couple who enjoys a joyful and rewarding relationship, it means they have struggled to make it that way. You see, when God created the institution of marriage, he at once gave us the option of finding within it the greatest joys known and the most thrilling life possible, or life's bitterest disappointments and most anguished moments. The degree to which you attain the high ideals you have set for your marriage depends to a large extent upon your willingness to work toward that end.

Unfortunately there are no easy formulas to guarantee happiness. However, you can go a long way on the words of the psalmist: "Blessed is every one who fears the Lord, who walks in his ways! You shall eat the fruit of the labor of your hands; you shall be happy, and it shall be well with you." Psalm 128:1-2

Now if you take those words to heart it doesn't mean that you will "live happily ever after." The Christian home is not immunized against the dissension and problems which afflict normal relationships. But worshiping Christ in the home does provides a basis for love, and fosters a willingness to forgive, that lends itself to harmony and reconciliation.

So I strongly urge you, _____ and _____, to establish a period of devotions in your new home. From experience I can tell you that time set aside for Bible reading and prayer has done much to unite our home. I find that I cannot harbor ill feelings against my wife and family when I listen to God's Word for me and must, in turn, pray for Christ's blessings on them. All disharmony disappears before the healing love of Christ. I hope you begin a family altar from day one, because the longer you wait, the greater the probability that your marriage will never be enriched by this wonderful time of prayer and meditation.

Another thing the psalmist gently suggests is that we do not take life and its blessings for granted. The God who created the world at its beginning is still in the business of creation. To him belongs the glory and honor for home and work, for family and food. It is important that we do not recieve these gifts thoughtlessly. Therefore I encourage you to be wise stewards of any and all blessings which God showers upon you. Frequent attendance at worship can be a continual reminder that Jesus is Lord and you are dependent upon him, not only for your daily material needs, but for your spiritual well-being and emotional stability as well.

I don't say these things to you because that's what a pastor should say to a couple on their wedding day. I share these words because I know them to be true.

I have a sister who lives in suburban Minneapolis, in a neighborhood in which church-going is not a priority. Yet, when her neighbors are upset or troubled, they run to my sister and her husband, to a home which is built on the strong foundation of faith in Christ. The persons who come to them for help don't like to recognize it is Jesus which makes this home such a refuge, but that is precisely what makes it special. The home which has Jesus as its cornerstone is built on a strong foundation which can stand secure amid even the most perilous storms of life.

You will need that kind of foundation for your marriage, _____ and _____. And so, as you leave to begin your life together, I remind you of these cheerful words: blessed you will be, _____ and _____, if you hold the Lord in awe and walk in his ways. You shall eat the fruit of labor of your hands. You shall be happy; and it shall be well with you.

That is our prayer. God bless you both. Amen

The Goal of Marriage

(Name) and __(name)__, what is happening today may not be taking place exactly as you had envisioned. But believe me, your days of reverie are over. Reality is here. Today you become man and wife. What a privilege it is, and what a joy we feel, to share this special and sacred hour with you.

Since this is reality and not some romantic fantasy, we must speak to you about life as it is. There's a telling passage in Shaw's play, "Back to Methuselah," which can get us started. Adam and Eve are talking to the serpent. Adam says, "I will live a thousand years and then I will endure no more. I will die and take my rest, and I will love Eve all that time, and no other woman."

Eve says, "If Adam keeps his vow, I will love no other man until I die."

The serpent says, "You have just invented marriage. And what he will be to you and not to any other woman is husband. And what you will be to him and not to any other man is wife."

Adam says, *"Husband and wife."*

Eve says, *"Wife and husband."*

And the serpent laughs, because he knows that the trouble has already started.

Well, the troubles of men and women have multiplied since then, and most of the problems are far more serious than who gets top billing on the *marquee of marriage*. In truth, because of our self-centeredness every one of us fails to live up to God's ideals for marriage.

That's why even back in Jesus' day (a time, in some ways, not so different from our own) problems in marriage and easy divorce were commonplace. In fact, Jewish law permitted a man to divorce his wife very easily. A man, for instance, could justifiably get rid of his wife if she burned his food or put too much salt on it. He could divorce her if she went out in public without covering her head, talked with men in the streets, or talked back to her in-laws. It was against this background that Jesus spoke his immortal words, saying the only reason the Law permitted divorce was because men were, literally, *slow learners.* Matthew 19:8 He continues: "Haven't you read the scripture that says that in the beginning the Creator made people male and female? [His design was that] the two will become one. So they are no longer two, but one. Man must not separate, then, what God has joined together." Matthew 19:4-6 (Good News Version) When God instituted marriage he intended male and female to be one. So they are no longer to be regarded as two, but one. Therefore let no one separate what God has united.

Jesus reminded the people that God designed marriage to be a union of body, mind, and spirit, so the marriage partners become bonded into a single organism. This is not only a matter of sensual, romantic love, which in itself can be very beautiful. It is not just a matter of friendship and companionship which are, of course, essential. It is a matter of seeing the other as an extension of one's self — desiring for our mate all that we want for ourself. It means, therefore, to be willing to *work* — to do what is necessary — to bring happiness to our spouse.

In very practical terms it means, _____ and _____, you are going to have to live out your love and your commitments to each other in very mundane, everyday kinds of ways. You're going to have to be faithful to each other in all areas of your life. If your relationship is going to grow you will need to be open and honest with each other, willing to admit mistakes, and always ready to forgive. Indeed, as theologian, Gibson Winter, says, "Forgiveness is the daily bread of married life." If your marriage is going to survive, you will need to be patient and compassionate with each other. In other words — and it should be obvious by now — it's going to take dedication, devotion, and a lot of hard work, but it can be a labor of love.

It seems many couples work hard to foster a relationship during courtship, but once they become married they tend to take that relationship for granted. Perhaps that is why the Beatles' song of years ago is still relevant. The words ask, "Will you still need me; will you still feed me; when I'm sixty-four?" It's an important question; a lot of the fears people have regarding marriage revolve around questions like that.

That's why Jesus' words are so important, so necessary for us (for you) to take to heart. God intends that you should be able to relax in your love and in the commitments of your vows, and so be able to celebrate your marriage with unconditional enthusiasm. It is in the climate of total commitment showered liberally with unselfish love that you truly become one, as Jesus says, and your marriage becomes an exquisitely beautiful thing which grows more priceless as the years pass.

_____ and _____, that's the hope we have for you today. We know it's your desire as well, and it's a worthy goal. May you stay close to our Lord, that he might bless you and fill you with his power and grace, that the hopes and dreams of all of us for your marriage can become a wonderful reality, now and forever. Amen

Christian Love

There is no doubt, __(Name)__ and __(name)__, that today you are among the happiest people on the face of the earth, and for good reason. The love which you have tenderly nourished day after day is now being publicly celebrated as you enter the sacred estate of marriage.

If I were to ask why you wanted to pledge lifelong devotion to each other, you might respond, "Because we love each other."

But what is love? I ask because the word has so many definitions. We hear people say they love their husband or wife, but they also love their pets, or they just love mink coats, or they love to swim, but they *really* love ice cream. Some speak of loving God, or making love, or even yearning for love. Is the emotion behind the word *love* the same in each instance? Or is there something about the love involved in marriage which is unique?

The ancient Greeks had six different words which in English can be translated *love*. There was one love, however, which exceeded all others, a love which was pure, and powerful, and worth pursuing. It was called *agape*, or God's love. It is also called Christian love, because this kind of love can be fostered and developed. It is described by Paul in 1 Corinthians 13.

Now *agape* is not the kind of love you "fall in to." It does not come naturally like falling off a log. This love will not make one's knees a little weak when his beloved comes into view; it is not the sentimental love of popular songs. *Agape*, Christian love, affects more than our emotions. It involves our whole being, and is able to provide a basis for a long, hearty, and joyful marriage.

Paul lists fifteen characteristics of *agape:* Christian love. Let's look at a few and relate them to marriage.

Love is patient. That patience is a difficult virtue to come by is illustrated in the well-known prayer, "Lord, give me patience — right now!" Christian love thinks before it speaks and pauses before it acts. In our relationships we need to remember how patient God is with us — how he stands ready to forgive and pour out his love, in spite of the fact that we're often rebellious and not very lovable.

So pray for patience. It is the embryo of compassion, and it will give to your home the warm glow of kindness.

Love does not insist on its own way. This is a hard saying, because we are all inclined to want to get our own way. But marriage requires that we recognize our mate is accustomed to getting his or her way, too. So we recall our God who did not count the cost but gave his Son for us all.

In love you should follow God's example and willingly lay aside your own whims and desires, in order that harmony might reign in your home. No matter how much pride is swallowed in the process, it is a small price to pay for the joy it creates and the peace it brings.

Love keeps no score of wrong. Paul is telling us that the power of Christian love should be so strong it will not let anything overcome it. If we are offended or hurt, we should again use God's love as a pattern. Once we repent and ask for forgiveness, God cancels that sin and never brings it up again.

In your marriage, mistakes and hurts which are forgiven should be banished from conversation. Don't store up wrongs in your memories. It only leads to brooding and unhappiness. Rather, concentrate on the good your mate does; enumerate his or her redeeming virtues. And don't forget to thank God for those wonderful attributes which are so easy to take for granted. Let the offenses go and don't forget to be grateful.

There is no limit to the faith, hope, and endurance of love. Throughout a lifetime there are many problems, anxieties, disappointments, and sorrows. But a relationship which develops the qualities of which Paul speaks can meet, face to face, all that life flings at them. The love which bears all things confronts obstacles, not with calm resignation, but with triumphant fortitude. Christian love *can* overcome anything because it is not a feeling, it is the power of God within us -- and with God all things are possible.

_____ and _____, the love which you bear for each other and which today is made holy by God's blessing is his great gift as you begin your wedded life. Nourish this gift by dedicating yourselves to each other and by praying a loving Father for the strength to love each other with the same kind of love with which Christ loves you. Amen

The Joy of New Beginnings

(Name) and _(name)_, what a lovely way to begin the new year. Each New Year's Day stands as a milestone, marking opportunities for new beginnings. You two are doing this New Year's in a big way. You have come to this sanctuary with beloved family members and faithful friends, to share with them the sacred moments when you declare your love and promise before God to live as husband and wife for the rest of your lives.

You are embarking on a brand new adventure of life. It *will* be an adventure, I assure you, with surprises, problems, victories, and the wonder which is a part of every new undertaking. Although your love has been nurtured for some time, marriage marks a change in your relationship. You can throw away all your old maps; the territory you are entering is unexplored. And since it is a new beginning, it is at once both exciting and threatening.

There is the excitement of *your* home, and *your* things, and *your* love, and all the great experiences you share as you create your own traditions.

But there are also question marks. Question marks arise because we humans are an unpredictable lot. We can never know for sure how the other person will react, or even how we'll react. We really cannot know how things will work out.

This insecurity about the future reminds me of a story. A man was filing for divorce. The judge asked him, "Sir, on your wedding day, didn't you promise to stay with your wife, 'for better, for worse'?"

"Yeah," the man responded, "but you can't hold me to that."

"Why not?" the judge inquired.

"Well," replied the man, 'because, before I was married I

had no idea how bad 'worse' could be."

It's true. Before we make a commitment we don't know how two lives are going to blend. That's why beginnings are always threatening. Any beginning — a new relationship, a new home, a new community, a new job — every new beginning holds the potential for great joy or crushing disappointment. So today, _____ and _____, you are taking a risk as you face the beginning of marriage with all its possibilities "for better, for worse."

As ominous as that may sound, I have some good news for you: Jesus says, "Behold, I make all things new." Revelation 21:5 Because our Lord continually brings newness, it means that life, even with all its question marks, can be something to look forward to. He can take people and re-create them. He can take a life and remake it. He can take a hurt and heal it. He can take a severed relationship and restore it: make it new again! Wherever Jesus goes he brings newness, replacing the past with exciting possibilities for the future.

_____ and _____, we do not know what the future holds for you. We have, of course, our dreams that you will find a shared life of great joy with a minimum of friction and antagonism. We pray that you will fulfill each other's expectations of what it means to be a husband and wife and that you will find a life of wedded bliss. We hope you are spared serious illness or tragedy and that your way spreads out before you smoothly all the days of a long and happy life together.

Those are our dreams, but we know better. We know that no one escapes the trials, problems, and frustrations of life. And when you encounter them, it will be a great comfort to those of us who love you to know that you have invited Christ into your marriage. If he is your guide, then no matter what happens, we know there will always be the possibility of reconciliation, always the opportunity for newness, always the prospects for healing and celebration.

So, _____ and _____, with Christ, the beginnings you face together need not be so threatening, because you know that even if you fail, God is there to forgive. When you stumble, our Lord is at hand to lift you up. Should you tremble before tragedy, the Holy Spirit is present to shelter you under his wing and to gift you with great courage. For all the situations of life, for all of life's beginnings, the strong promise of Christ is that he will make all things new.

What a wonderful promise for you to live in as you begin this new year! What a great gift God gives you to share not only on your wedding day but for all the years of your life together.

We, your family and friends, pray for you, _____ and _____. We pray that our Lord will walk with you throughout the whole of your marriage and that he will daily add his newness to your relationship. So, as you walk from this place into the adventure of tomorrow, be assured you do not walk alone. Our Lord walks with you and our love surrounds you. May you seek the joys of Christ's newness in all the beginnings of your life. Amen

76

Notes

Notes

Notes

About the Author

John M. Braaten is Pastor of Administration at Bethel Lutheran Church, Rochester, Minnesota. He served previously at Mayville and Gran Lutheran Parish, Mayville, North Dakota, as well as in congregations at Boyceville, Wisconsin, and Fargo, North Dakota. A graduate from Luther College, Decorah, Iowa and Luther Theological Seminary (now Luther-Northwestern) in Saint Paul, Minnesota, he has done advanced study at the University of North Dakota and Luther-Northwestern Seminary. He is on the clergy roster of The American Lutheran Church.

In addition to his parish activities, pastor Braaten has frequently served as a seminar and workshop leader in education and worship for the district.

Pastor Braaten and his wife Julie, a microbiologist, are the parents of two sons and a daughter.